TO YOUR
SCATTERED
BODIES GO

TO YOUR
SCATTERED
BODIES GO

BRIAN BRETT

EXILE editions

singular fiction, poetry, nonfiction, translation, drama, and graphic books

Library and Archives Canada Cataloguing in Publication

Title: To your scattered bodies go / Brian Brett.
Names: Brett, Brian, author.
Description: Poems.
Identifiers: Canadiana (print) 20200279114 | Canadiana (ebook)
    20200279203 | ISBN 9781550968897 (softcover) | ISBN 9781550968903
    (EPUB) | ISBN 9781550968910 (Kindle) | ISBN 9781550968927 (PDF)
Classification: LCC PS8553.R387 T6 2020 | DDC C811/.54—dc23

Copyright © Brian Brett, 2022
Book designed by Michael Callaghan
Typeset in Granjon font at Moons of Jupiter Studios
Cover photograph *Perseus* (from the series *Diamond Nights*) by Beth Moon
Published by Exile Editions
144483 Southgate Road 14, Holstein, Ontario, N0G 2A0
www.ExileEditions.com
Printed and bound in Canada by Imprimerie Gauvin

We gratefully acknowledge the Canada Council for the Arts,
the Government of Canada, the Ontario Arts Council, and
Ontario Creates for their support toward our publishing activities.

Canadian sales representation: The Canadian Manda Group,
664 Annette Street, Toronto ON M6S 2C8.
www.mandagroup.com 416 516 0911

North American and international distribution, and U.S. sales:
Independent Publishers Group, 814 North Franklin Street,
Chicago IL 60610 www.ipgbook.com toll free: 1 800 888 4741

for Sharon, always

I

Interlude

II

I

TO YOUR SCATTERED BODIES GO

"At the round earth's imagin'd corners, blow
Your trumpets, angels, and arise, arise
From death, you numberless infinities
Of souls, and to your scattered bodies go."
— John Donne, *Holy Sonnets*

And I awoke in the thunder of those trumpets,
the bright lights and the sirens of the ass-slappers,
and I was but one of many awakenings, stars
numberless and bright beyond the galaxies,
human and insect, striving and writhing,
as we came tumbling over the walls
where we returned, tumbling again, full of arrows
and bulbuls and radiation, all of us loving
and dying in our gentled beds, hands held
by many fingers and the gaze of love, tumbling
into light and rivers, dodging crocodiles and not
dodging crocodiles; to your scattered bodies go
and then shrug them off in the Magellanic cloud
and the Mindanao deep, life going way back
to the big bang, and the bang we don't hear,
the one that strikes the heart and the lung and perforates
our spine as we crazy dance into the trenches of lovers
and weeping children, playing children, lost children,
the scattered bodies of seasons and life, like pearls
in the night sky, appearing and disappearing in the fog.

THE RAIN ON THE RED TIN ROOF

The rain on the tin roof, it makes
me feel hunted, makes me feel like a tiger
in Singapore, before there was a Singapore,
before I realized I'd reached six decades.
The rain on the red tin roof comes down
in waves, in an excess of climate.
I love the way it dances its rich weather.
Rain on the roof, as sweet as a slim, shy
girl slipping off her wet sheath under
the bridge in my twentieth year.
After that, only the rain spoke.

KNIFE DREAM

Though not a gypsy, his gypsy camp
was off the road, in the woods,
his cowboy hat perched on a twig.
The handmade forge glowing
from the jury-rigged bellows.
I brought him whittled pear wood,
and he hauled out a big file.
"It's super-hardened steel," he said
with some reverence as he tossed
it into the fire, and began the forging,
the rhythmic beat on the anvil, the folding
in the radiance of the dusky woods.

This is my killing knife, rough and sharp,
the shape I imagined for throat-slitting
the big buck or the extra ram, good also
for skinning and boning. Brass-riveted
pear-wood-handle bound with shrunken thongs,
the case sewn out of a mean old steer's hide cured
with country skill to sheathe a country knife.

THE MANY MOMENTS

When I think of the dirt
     I'm going to eat,
the dust I will become, the mud
flowing along the ocean floor,
     I wonder
where those great moments of a life
          go—
the inspired pauses that "Haw!!"
in the face of what most would call reality.

The moments where even the glass-eyed geek
dances on the ruin of those who foiled him.

     When we die,
our families spend the rest of their lives
     forgetting us,
the way we forget the dog licking knives
     in the dishwasher,
the bicycle dance of the courier in traffic.
We leave nothing behind but energy—
entropy into organism into entropy.

Go then, now,
to the star's core,
the tree's leaf,
the raven's betrayed squawk.
You can find our ragged essence everywhere,
translated.

BLACKBERRIES, THEY MAKE

Blackberries, they make
life, they make summer
into sugar, they make a thatch
that humus-thickens the earth
rich if you can clear the brambles.

Plucked and bloody I have
wandered your thorns, my eyebrows
slashed, fingers dark stained.
Like the ancient purple-faced
mythic whore of Babylon,
I am inside my life and hunger.

Blackberries, they make
seedy jam and lush pies,
they make fine juice, or a port
fermented in vats and jugged
and drunk among slurry friends
determined to headache the dawn.

Blackberries, they bring
the family together in the field,
trampling, sampling, camping;
the whole goddamned number,
almost numberless actually, and if the summer
is hot and the rains come in August, briefly,
the berries fatten like black thumbs in the green
thorns, humming with bears
and greedy children like me.
"Watch out for that huge hive of bees,"
my brother said, about the last words
I remember before I accidentally shoved
the branch into the nest and the chocolate
bumblebees came pouring over my head,
while I ran screeching into the field toward
the deep fluorescent slime of the ditch;
shouting, screaming, scrambling, scattering
the purple-hearted sweetness of summer.

THE SINGERS

I've been lucky enough to hear
a woman sing her desire
        several times.
One gave me an opera
when I penetrated her
and I was so surprised
my desire softened,
but only for a moment.
Then she sang the songs
while we made the music of love.
Then there was the woman in the hotel room;
we never met, yet every grunt and woof and trill
in the room above me—her Arctic cocoon—
transformed my sleepless and hungry night
until it was rich with the memory of lost desires.

And another—the last—lovely, frail, and just met—
        then she disappeared—
taking her choice of a different man by the hand
to the bedroom where she cried out so loudly,
        it hurt.

THE LAST THRUSH

Will he? Will this man-thing ever hear
the haunt of the Swainson's thrush
again in another wide summer to come?
He's a walking wound walking,
He's the mortar and pestle of busted joints;
the crippled dog under the willow;
the withering plums almost too sweet;
the drooping breasts of the wry, old girl;
the wind in autumn showing its scarlet bottom,
prancing its leafy whirl-a-whirl
and the haunted songs of invisible
birds celebrating the dusk.
Hoohoo sweet, sweet, the enduring birds sing.

ENDLESS LOVE AND ROSES

A lonely man in a public garden.
These are the roses of the dead,
the roses of the living,
the roses of the lovers
bathing in their perfume.
He walks past the lush red *Lincoln*
under a sign in a slab of stone.
Tuum est—it is yours.
Yes, desire is always ours.
The roses go on forever,
the *Peace,* blowsy and as
overblown as its era.
The local lovers slide like eels
over each other's bodies in the corners
of the garden. They are kissing, fondling,
twining. It's almost a cartoon of love,
blessed by the eagerness of the young.

The lonely man notices another in a corner—
thin, and attractive, his shoulders
angular—pretty despite his own pain—
a blond sorrow framed by the *Damasks*,
and then the lonely man walks
toward becoming human again.

THE GREAT WHITE WHALE

He surfaced suddenly on the beach, my dad
sliding out of his shirt and pants,
straps and braces and belly bands of brown
leather, tossing the wooden leg aside,
standing suddenly in his white shorts,
his white body, his one white leg.
Then he hopped beyond his clothing,
hopping on that leg the twenty steps
to the beach, the powerful leg
like a fin casting off from the land
and then he was leaping sideways to the sky,
with the joy of a white whale, its body glowing
in the air before it cut back into the water
of the lake; then surfaced, blowing, my father,
the bright whale, the only one to see
that Uncle Rocco was drowning, even before
Rocco knew he wasn't going to touch land,
but the whale circled underwater in one
smooth arc, and the whale came up roaring
between Rocco's legs and hurled them both
shoreward, where land embraced Rocco again
and he spit out all the water he'd swallowed
while my father, whalelike, circled out there;
secretly proud and as silent as a whale,
he left the crying and shouting to the relatives.

THE CLOTHING OF MY YOUTH

I want to wear the clothes
I wore when I thought
I was a pretty boy, when pretty
was a fantasy within reach—
the purple pants, skin-tight
except for the flaring bell-bottoms.

The pink shirt, frilled with peasant sleeves,
the frills also fluttering down my chest.
The Edwardian cape, the poncho, grey and brown—
made of the best dog hair;
the subtle colour, the texture....
The vain little boy shining in his soft armour.

These outfits were a surface
on my teenage anguish—
the blue jean jacket embroidered
with the half-complete phoenix
(how I loved its promised whole),
the beige corduroy, pseudo blue jeans,
their paisley and leather bell-bottom
gussets capturing wind and space.

This was when men believed
they could peacock in the world.
Today, the dullness is upon them, shaved,
baggy, indiscriminate, hidden, lost.
Fashion that brags of its fake poverty
dusted with tasteless gangster bling?
I hope not. Yet I want to have the choice
between a world without shape and colour,
and the rich surface of brilliant designs
        that ornament our lives.

TALL TALES

My father was made of stories, and his myths
lived alongside reality, as fathers always do.

You are dead ten years and I still
want to sit on your lap and be tortured.
I remember when you got into the wine
and the whisker-rubs almost
scraped the skin off my cheeks,
how you tormented me with laughter;
then took me to your legendary kingdoms
where the shipyard rivets glowed in the night sky
as your tongs flung them to the man on the destroyer,
and the mattress factory was afloat with feather down
while everyone coughed bright red blood,
or when you scored a half-ton of copper pipe for the junker.
    The giant octopus was always
      dragging your boat sideways;
the shark swimming away with your amputated leg.
You made my world into your myths; archetypal—chthonic
    stories for the child I forever became.

THE SUMMER OF MY FATHER

"Il faut cultivar son jardin."
—Voltaire, *Candide*

I would like to have
this one last summer
before I die, my father
said with his simple honesty,
and then he died
on a brilliant day in May.
And now twelve years later
I am down on my knees,
my hands riffling the black earth,
ripping out the morning
glory roots and quack grass.
The beans are so tall
in the heat their poles
are bending toward me
like unkempt, silent priests.
The thyme is humming with bees.
This is the garden in its glory.
Yet my joints hurt so bad
that I will have trouble standing
again in the light flooding
upwards from the sea,

because the hornet of death is now
singing in my blood as I live
this last summer of my father.

THE BONES ARE ROTTEN

On a morning like too many mornings
you wake up again knowing
that every dawn in your future
will be signalled by your near luminous
      embrace of pain.

Pain is the gift of your last days.
The one constant. Pain. Good pain.
The reminder that the thrill
of the years of walking over mountains
      demands a companion.

You gotta pay if you're gonna play.
Bird songs outside, pain songs inside.
The flake-crackling joints
teach you to celebrate
the hurt gifts of the morning.

OUR REPTILE FACE

The red racer has a green tree frog
in her mouth, and the frog
embraces the snake.
Their jaws are locked.
Death is inevitable
and they stare at each other
with reptile eyes,
the frog aware of the end,
yet struggling for position—
the power of the frog
can't match the snake,
but still they fight.

Like this tranquil frog—
how many among us
wouldn't bite the face
that marks our fate,
and wrestle our giants
until they swallow us?

EVERY DOG WANTS TO LIVE

A found poem based on a now lost newspaper article.

Dosha,
　　　　let out to piss
on the green lawn
　　　　　　　　jumped the fence
and was run over
　　　on Olympic Drive.
And only cut her nose, standing stunned
when the cop, Badge 123,
　　　　came up and shot her,
because he didn't have time to deal
　　　　with this kind of thing.
She was taken down to Public Works,
and they put her in the freezer
　　　　for two hours,
because they also didn't know what to do with her—
　　　Dosha—cut and shot.

When they went to transfer her to the dump
she was standing at the door, wounded and bleeding,
wagging her tail with the joy of the alive.

THE SHINING TERNS

The terns came yesterday
bright and white, cocked wings
pulled back, arching, as they dipped,
skimming the lake beyond the deck.

Every night I lie down
and wonder what I will
leave behind in the mist
of this lake and these terns.

No more, maybe less
than they will carry south
into the jungles of their adventures,
while I sleepwalk my own journey
toward a winter that won't end.

THE SHORT, NATURAL HISTORY
OF A WALKER

We're walking, yes, we're walking;
it's a variety of dancing, it's the source
of poetry. I've dreamed so much language
walking Rimbaud's glittering trail of the Great Bear—
my big, crippled foot close to my heart—
the poem that infected my younger years.

Once, in 1972, I walked across Mexico City.
It was one of my great walks.
I was so alive on those narrow roads
and in those barrios, as much
as I was alive in the grandiosity
of the broad avenues that led to the square
where they shot the students, and to Chapultepec,
the home of the sunstone—
       that carved circle
       a calendar, a fate that
       time walks around.

THE BLUE SNOWSUIT

Fifty years ago, the snowsuit was
the newest thing since Wonder Bread
which was white, fluffy, and sliced.
The real wonder of the bread
was that it took the wheat out of the wheat
in an age when people were impressed
by food that didn't feed.
The snowsuit was blue,
and there was snow then, lots of it.
My mother would tirelessly put on
my layers of bundling underclothes
and zip me into my blue suit,
the little boots, the little gloves,
and I would rush out into the snow
as white as Wonder Bread,
and eat it without peanut butter or jam.
Then I would grow cold and cry
at the door, and mother would
let me inside and take off layer
after layer, like peeling a bright little onion
who was crying in discomfort.
But after a few minutes with the fireplace
and a slice of bread and jam I would
cry and cry and cry until mother

bundled me up again and sent
me back out into the world of wonder.
I was so young then and already
I failed to understand the need
for the borders we call doors
that shut in and shut out
the wonders of the other side.

MUTANT CHILD'S STORY

It used to be that when mutant children
like me were born deformed, they were left
out in the rain to die.

Now I walk in the world,
with the hard cinder of my sorrow
burnt into my chest.

And though I walk in the lustre
of the world, I understand why
they used to leave my kind to die—
because every day has some rain
and the suffering is without end.

THIRTY YEARS AFLAME

When we meet our bodies
slide, the wet skin slippery
with love and desire touching,
unconscious already, disappeared—
love is all there is and we dive
into the darkness and the clutch—
our hands on fire, our heads
on fire, the church of our flesh
      on fire.

KILL ME NOW

"Short our end and minish our pain;
Let us go and never come again."
　　　　　　　　　—Everyman

The light goes both ways, darkness
leading to light as much as light goes dark.
We've had our summer in the sun
and now it is time to hunger the dark.

Kill me quick, kill me with the gun,
or the sweet sleep of exotic narcotics.
Kill me. Kill me, so that I can die
the way I lived because dying is
merely the ultimate form of living
in the sudden thrill of the moment.

I'll take the violent suicide express, or
I'll take the quiet of the heart murmuring,
the exhaustion of that final, slow breath.

WHEN TIME WAS FOREVER

Don't you miss those forever days at the beach,
reading enormous books, and watching
acrobatic children play their crazy age,
and the near-naked women and men
proud walking under the sun?

Time had no end then, life flowed everywhere,
memory and hope lived side by side,
until hope moved on, until time changed time.

TURKISH DELIGHT

Lovers through the centuries,
flesh born and born again,
fat and muscle and desire,
over and over, unexplained
we find each other
in the joke of a gift of candy.

We lie down together in cemeteries.
We kiss beside train stations.
We touch and touch again; O how
I have known the fullness of your body
without ever penetrating it.

The kiss beside the tracks,
wrapped around each other,
my hands up your blouse
fondling your breasts and nipples
while the Turks and Gypsies gawk
and flash high signs,
and guard us unconsciously
from thieves and thugs because love
is loved in every country.
We are only refugees in desire,
pouring sugar into our mouths,

protected in our privilege
by the homeless, poverty-struck
Turks and their sweet gifts.
We are free together, lost
in this exotic moment,
as the centuries of love and grace
are poured into a candied kiss.

THE SPANISH STEPS

"This living hand, now warm and capable
Of earnest grasping, would, if it were cold
And in the icy silence of the tomb,
So haunt thy days and chill thy dreaming nights."
                                        —John Keats

When I die I'm going to the Spanish Steps.
I'll rent a little room on the second floor
and look out the window at the stone barque below.

These are the widest stairs in Rome
but not as big as the dreams I exhaled,
my lungs rattling and spitting blood
in "the year of miracles," the year
of words that tilted the world,
nightingales and antique Greek urns,
following bright stars and a Darien peak,
the music of the earth never ceasing—
surprises that surprised even me
      during those few days
when I wrote them in a fever of phrases.

      There it is, the song,
      and after that I am gone.

The bureaucrats, frightened by my bloody lips,
will come with their torches and burn everything
after I coughed up my lungs with consumption.

> *The walls are on fire.*
> *the bed is on fire,*
> *that last window*
> *is forever on fire.*

And this window will make old poets
and children hush and show tears
in the centuries that follow, looking
down upon the stone boat of the dead.

Flaming walls follow the poets too often.
After me, here comes the wrecking crew.

THE WINNING

The days belong to us, and the nights,
and the burnished light in between.
It's a glory—the fields of molten corpses,
the morning meadow aflame with poppies.

Monkeys and seahorses and thistledown.
Sad dogs and lilies and gneiss rocks.
The foam on the pint of dark dark beer.
The organic earth of life.
The urban deserts called parking lots.
The flash of your eyes,
blue in the blue blue blue night.

Everything's born. Everything erodes.
The amoeba slithers across the glass.
The children cough and die, or laugh and cry.
All these lives are the prize, the one
called existence without qualifiers.
Every death rattle a battle hymn,
every breath a victory.

Interlude

WHAT'S THE POEM?

It's the weirdo in his nightgown,
    trimming the wick
    of an old-fashioned beeswax candle
and lighting a joint with a blowtorch.
    It's the shy girl straightening her hair
on the ironing board—with an iron.
        It's the poet in a suit with a career plan.
        It erupts everywhere.

It's you standing on the stage,
                    your feet slightly apart,
your weight centred on your solar plexus,
        your *chakra*,
        your little pot belly....
whatever in hell's name you want to call it—
            but it's centred.
And the voice comes out of the gut, a voice
            of power,
rising,
        rising,
            rising.
Quiet power,
            controlled
                and uncontrolled power,

loud sometimes,

           though not often.

Silence is much louder than a shout.

And sound came before the song.

The beat,

    the terrible beat of bones,

        and hands,

        and drums,

        and rocks,

        and power—

        the power,

        of rhythm.

    Start in a cave,

    solo in a skyscraper.

Grunt and flex and live and watch your lover die.

    Crash the cliff

    and kiss the demon.

Demean yourself, but not your friends.

    Sing,

    sing,

    sing,

and then sing again,
until you're ready to get it written.

Then you can form the first words like codes;
give those codes weight and symbols and substance.
Rhyme everything and then forget rhyme.

When you come out of the cave
you will squeak a little bit,
maybe croak like a frog,
but you will find your voice,
standing on the stage,
legs apart,
centred,
the sound rolling out
of your mighty chest—
full-breasted or breastless, sparrow-chested
or bodybuilder-boy—
that doesn't matter in the end,
only the voice like syrup and silence and birds
greeting the morning.

Sing like the butterfly's wing;
the shark;
the shy entrepreneur;

the slutty, big-toothed land developer
with his armload of environmental reports;
the annoyed secretary,
the pompous professor.
Sing like the fencepost in a flood.
Sing like the virgin at the orgy.

Kill adverbs and adjectives,
and then revive them with a kiss.
Know a good noun when you see it,
and the verb that needs no modifier.
Then ignore all advice,
except the one that demands:
these words
in this place!

Now you are ready to write the singing codes
some call poems,
poems of desire
that will be meaningless to most of us,
but grab the hearts of a few like an Aztec priest
in the magic of sacrifice.

It's easy.
Just do everything.
And then do it again,
only better,
and then again....

THE WRECK

The beautiful bodies remain;
it took me forty years to return
        to this beach,
the stairs enormous now, endless,
where once there weren't even stairs,
the downward flow toward water
        and sun,
and even more endless the return
past the grave beside the trail
of the girl who died too young
and is celebrated every year
by her "Wreck Beach Family."

        It's the naked
who made this place and held it
in the roar of an era when
we reached outside of ourselves,
naïvely, goofy, dancing—
naked, naked, beautifully naked.
        Clothing Optional.
As the government would have it
        after the fact,
on the standardized sign where nudity
is equal to dogs and parking and vending.

　　　　Ah well, Wreck Beach
lives beyond the bureaucracy that discovered
　　　　there were people down here,
singing their old songs—*margaritas, marijuana,*
mushrooms, organic juice, sarongs,
　　　　water, water, water....

The crescent of sand boiling
with bodies—life, in its variety;
attractive and red, fat women; slug-pale
men who resemble refugees
from starvation camps;
pot-bellied men and women—
small-dicked, big-dicked, the man
with testicles like bagged oranges—
the woman with the shaved, bird-winged pussy—
　　　　the pouch, the cleft, the hairy,
　　　　the purple panties—
small breasts, dangling pricks, the perky,
　　　　the floppy, the perfect.
We're all here, copper-coloured, black,
white, or striped scarlet and painful,
the gorgeous and the homely-gorgeous,
tattooed, pierced, and shining with oil—
the knob-knees, the six-pack abdomen,

the bumpy, shaved skull.
This is the body in its variety,
        clothed and unclothed,
and the minds that go with it,
the gawkers and the bored,
the stoned young men who bought
the mushrooms and dived into the mud,
        near the annoyed Canada Geese,
        painting themselves
        into a savage joke of mud
        and laughter, watered
        with a few beer
while their bikini-beautiful companions
        roll their eyes,
        displaying the patience
        of lovers under a hot sun.

        We must adore
        the truly relaxed,
the thick and the misshapen,
        though not the creep
        playing with himself
until someone asks him to leave,
        perhaps too politely.
The slim, flame-haired

woman with tiny breasts
          and endless legs—
the grace of a dancer.
The old, withered couple—
even their scars are tanned—
          sipping a good wine
          from crystal
they packed for at least a mile.

We approach The Wreck
          the way we arrived,
naked and lovely to the world.

CEDAR CHILD'S DREAM SONG

I opened my eyes in the moss
and saw that I was a blind seed.

Once I dreamed I was liquid
      running through the light-streaked shadows.
        Creation was after me,
                shouting,
   enticing,
        luring me with the sexy promise
   of another world,
        but I knew
      only this world, and I fell
into the moist womb of the green.

I was the strange one,
          beautiful
            in my strangeness.
I was the arborvitae, the *thuja plicatus*.
I first appeared in the Jurassic—
     wet   wet   wet   child
     of the wet world,
child of the neon green ravines.
Now the Nuu-chah nulth call
me *huu-mis, huu* the long lasting.

I was the broken one.
                    I snapped so hard,
          brittle in my resilience.
They left me in the forest.
                    They did that—left me.
     I grew extra legs.   I grew hollow,
I grew twisted, I grew against the grain.
          I was wood.

     Eagles offered the salmon god
     to my roots, decaying red in the rain forest.
     The silver-tip brought her belly-sucked
     brain-eaten gifts from the dark of the river.

I made a deadly
                    bed of needles, thujaplicin,
the poison where only the moss thrive
          and the mink hiss at the moon.

And the young, shaggy lovers
came afraid,   but came,   seeding decay
          between my roots and their legs.
Insects ran to the shore;
then growing, and returning,
as insect nature does, moved
from the egg to the skyscraper.

Then the crazy began,
              the user world,
                      history defined faster,
          faster and faster.

I am the halibut hook and a basket.
I am the roof and the wall and the wedge.
I am the fire and the incandescent kindling.
I am the hat and underpants and skirt.
I am the withes twisted into rope
that hauls the whale to the beach.
I am the baby's soft blanket.
I am the chuk-chuk-chuk of the adze
on the canoe and the bentwood box,
I am the boat and the box,
the paddle and the bailer.

I am the perfume, the fragrant bed.
I am the totem and the door.
I am the whistle and the rattle.
I am the spoonful of red red roe.
I am the house post that held
the festival of existence.
I am the plate and the bowl,
so now you can feed from my belly.

I am the board that shelters,
the roof that protects, the fence
that defends or corrals.
I am export and import,
raw log and finished wall.

The slime took me, the cell in the pool,
the hard,

        hard,

                soft,

                        softness of centuries,
mudded together with wind and water,
and salmon and chainsaws and log booms,
and salt-life rubbed to a glow with ratfish oil.
Call me Thunderbird and Raven Transforming
into a cabinet door or a clapper or a story
of fecundity rushing through the forest,

        the before and the after,
from first logic to gasoline,

                bracing against the storms
of the coast while rocks rise and the sea swells.

The child of winter,

                water,

                      cold,

              snow,
         slime,
     the dancing girl:
I'm the one,
       the survivor,
gold fleshed, deepening with age.
     I've been lustered.

     I've come through until now,
always, beside the stickleback pools,
       the scarlet green coho –
dusted with the eagle-down dancing
above the heads of the children
     as they begin
reconstructing our wounded planet.

SALMON CHILD'S RIVER CALL
after Al Purdy

Sister, the waters
    are good,
the waters are salt and cold,
and the magnetic north humming.

The sun went down on the banks,
and we reached the kelp beds,
and then the big water
where the whales and seals,
the dolphins, sea lions, and tuna,
the flickering mackerels,
snapped around us—
the lines and nets of the deep.
Sister, we have to swim for our lives
in the silver of our muscles.

Sister, I was the hunter, chasing
    the squid and the krill.
I ate the diatoms and the weeds
    and the young grilse,
but I never took more than I needed.

I never took more than I needed.

Then I returned to the river, *Sister*,
against the current, past the wide delta,
the wrecked shacks, the oil, the fumes,
the sour taste spilling out of the creeks.
Sister, this arsenical water is still our river,
despite the whiff of uranium and cyanide and PCBs;
this river is still ours, and we go glowing,
over the shallows, past the middens.
      The run of life,
      never quitting.

Shining with muscle and desire,
past the hairy paws of the bear
and the beak of the sudden eagle,
      I am here...
at the spawning country,
      what's called the redds.
In the milt,
      finning my grave,
crisp with light and cool water
where the shallows are clear

and the sun flashes golden through
the dappling alders and cedars.
Sister, where are you?
>*Sister...*
>>*Sister...?*

>Where are you?

FOOD CHAIN

A white moth on a trajectory
across the ornamental pond
does not understand nets and death,
except perhaps as abstract constructions—
the first strand less than an inch away,
or does it know the whole thread?—
history working, our past weaving
into snapshots, framed pictures, windows.
This one—
      the touch;
that one—
      the apple bough shivering;
then here it comes, weird,
the approach of the final horror of the night,
         the dancing arachnid.

She's hot and sensual, dusting your throat
with her fangs, measuring her meals
by smell and spider-leg-touch,
and you fight a lot at first,
         near the envelope
of the waterfall, where the underwater lamp makes drastic
      configurations on the oily surface.

It's a slickly designed pond in a rich man's house,
      breeding carp to enchant children,
      and displaying those flashy,
         spare-no-expense,
      lilies to impress clueless relatives.

Monstrous creatures, the carp, lie fat and full
in the mud of their lairs, like old bachelors
      or poachers,
stuffing everything into their maws,
until one day, out of nowhere, the osprey dives.

I was walking by at the lucky hour of midnight,
when chance let me witness
the death of a moth:
      a display of the spider's art spun
         from the geometry of its guts—
cultivated through a million years
of bad webs and evolutionary blind allies.
And I flushed with the memory of a girl
I knew when I was young, how she danced
her slender fingers all over my body,
That web was no worse than this one.
Even her family hated me, especially when

I was sucked dry.
and cast off like a snakeskin,
        a carcass in a ditch.
Grateful, I was, yet weeping over the loss.
Why do I always love the women who hurt?

Arachne, you wind your victims up
into bundles of jerking meat.
        It's the old history
of dinner and love and death
that swallows every creature.
I loved your stories about the fat ones,
how they took days to suck dry.

I wanted to learn your spider moves,
running on a tightrope to dinner.
But there are no survivors in that
        expensive, mood-lit pond
of brand identifications, the sleek BMW nearby.

I never enjoyed the advertising:
        the biggest web,
        the whitest wings,
        the perfect story,
except for those that perish, dehydrated

near black-water lily pads,
while the spider dances her victory
music plucked on the silk she so elegantly spun.
        She is the queen of the discos
and coffee bars—you can meet her wearing
a nose ring at Alberto's. She is everywhere,
        our lady of the living lunch,
sticking us with her ancient poisons.

She skitters so excitedly on the line,
folding up the moth as if it were a suitcase,
while the memory stings and I pause in the dark,
        watching a moth
trapped in a shimmering web—
        a spider dancing a kill, a savage
        contest of flesh, riding
the surface tension between chaos patterns.
I've seen the same show in the divorces of several friends:
        sometimes male, sometimes female.
Actually, Arachne,
the spider is in either sex.
        Call it arachnid,
today a woman, tomorrow a man, Tuesday
        a body in between. It's not which sex
                but the sexy descent.

Don't you remember it, again and again,
the knot of desire and the little deaths,
the delighted pounce, and the moth rolled up?
Are you the one eating,
or the one being eaten?

Then they freeze, poised on the net,
moth and spider,
shivering above the water,
captured in the light of the lamp,
two dancers locked into the night of their lives,
gazing at the open jaws
as the red carp rises....

THE CONTROL SHOT *(Kontrolnyi Vystrel)*

The *kontrolnyi vystrel*
     comes on its own wind, comes to her
who feeds her mother and weeps on weekends,
     comes to her who interviews
an old lady slit open like a chicken on a table.
     "They gutted me," the crone said
before sliding into morphine's kingdom—
     intent on her slow and sloppy decline.
Then the journalist went home and gathered
     her groceries at the elevator to heaven.
The kind man invited her in, shot her a few times
     and while she was regurgitating
     among the apples and the yogurt
injected the *kontrolnyi vystrel* into her brain.
     That's a slug shredded
to expand like an egg thrown against a wall.
Soon she is spasming and shitting herself,
     but fortunately, unconscious,
because she is dead and her electric body
     hasn't recognized that yet.

It was during the winter of dead writers
     that I found myself in the field.
And the waning moon was hooked in a dying cedar—

half a moon, half a cedar,
echoing the pasture of the dead grass,
        the kingdom of history,
the climate changing at the end
of this grassland, the stricken cedars morphing,
dying, replaced by dryland madrona and fir trees.
I was kicking dirt at my useless life
        and the lambs were larking
because they thought dirt was a game
        and any dance meant joy.
        They hadn't yet seen the waltz
        of the cadaver on the line—
after the hammer hit the brain, while the skinner
        considers the twitching corpse.

These journalists, these activists, they discovered
        such fantastical ways to die.
        Please let me jump off that railing.
        I spent my life telling my community
        about all the crimes against them,
so now I'm depressed, on the eve of my big story,
        and I think I'll kill myself, messily—
        that pumpkin hitting the sidewalk,
well, that was my head because I hated myself
and not the enemies of my neighbours and family.

And don't you dare ask why we are dying.
You could have an "allergic reaction" to life,
        or be shot dead in your office.
        Dying is easy. Protesting is hard.
        Don't go to football matches.
        Don't live relaxed in this world.
And don't walk the busy streets where everybody walks.
        An entire volley of control shots,
        not just the necessary one, were delivered
        to the honest cop who believed he could walk
        with other cops. This is spectacle,
        the miracle of the street.
Did his companions dust the route of the assassins,
        like curlers polishing the ice of murder?
They didn't get a chance to see the faces of the killers
        because they were too busy clearing
        his path to the bounty of the honest.
But what about the polonium in the tea another critic drank.
        Yes, death is original,
        especially in a foreign nation,
        since it's apparently legal to slow-murder
those "enemies of the Russian regime"
and leave a radioactive trail through the bodies
        of bystanders and hotel rooms.
This is wild stuff. This is extreme murder.

It's so crazy it must be fun for the faceless suits
        wandering through the hotel rooms
of the world with their guns and radiation and balconies.
        Originality is always rewarded.
 But getting noticed means the *kontrolnyi vystrel*.
        That's the law of the urban war,
that's why the children in the school will die,
becoming examples of discipline, the right path,
        the exploding basketball court,
        the body parts
whizzing out of the windows and roof and doors.
        They were running everywhere,
 the wounded children, the parents dervished
        with panic, the teacher holding
        a thumb missing a hand; hell, where's
the rest of that delicate child, those tiny fingers—
        the whole bleeding body
        is gone, or bowing in the courtyard,
        headless and handless, praying
to the unknown god of death's circuitry
that makes corpses twitch long after
the life has exploded in glorious flame
        into an unutterably blue sky.
They blew up a few apartments while they were at it.
        Planted some traces of mystery.

Made the visible invisible.
The world needs control, and murder
is the best control, the *kontrolnyi vystrel*,
        the method of methods, the miracle.

        My darling, my darling,
they are killing our friends around the world.
        Let me lie in your arms,
holding your rich, naked body against mine
because I am cancered with these deaths,
        and I don't want to live any more.
Animated in the never-ending cycle where
the daily record includes the bodies draped
over theatre seats, those scarved women
        gassed and shot,
their bellies pregnant with explosives and patriotism,
while secret agents smoked cigarettes on the street
        as the lovers of opera were carted
to oblivion, their lungs full of state secrets,
        the ultimate theatre, fatal,
inscrutable, disguised and costumed,
        the double meaning of bullets.
The dead are everywhere, handless embracers
        of blood diamonds, or choked
        with dust in the forever wars,

cringing in the jungles, merely blood spatters
　　　　after the doors blew off the nightclub,
　　　　legless storytellers of the landmines
of Afghanistan exploding in the opium fields,
　　　　child soldiers with big guns,
　　　　booksellers in the Baghdad market—
　　　　no nation owns the luxury
of the dead children in the basketball court,
　　　　the executed truth speakers.
　　　　Every cadaver is personal.
The memories hang like chains from my hair
　　　　when I walk down the street,
my lungs rattling, almost yearning for the morphine
　　　　which will silence me as exquisitely
　　　　as the guardians of the regimes
with their guns and knives and plastic explosives
　　　　and extraordinary extraditions,
　　　　and that's also why tomorrow,
someone, somewhere, will gather up
the gear of survival and silently, sweetly,
leave for the distant, green hills at dawn.

II

DIVIDERE

In Italy the lovers at a table
mingle fingers, and offer morsels
to the other's tongue, sharing the dish.
It's called *dividere*, and when you request
this charm of dividing love's desire,
you get two plates of one for two—
the waiters understand, and divide
the dishes we love, with tenderness.

We are old now, my dear,
but we eat like young romantics,
and lick our fingers and each other's
lips and tongues and plates.

We ate everything.
My *pasta polpo,* octopus in Aosta,
or your *pasta con funghi,*
with its creamy mushrooms—
Asinello di latta arrosto—
that surprise we were served in Matera.
Nobody told us its horror—a baby donkey
nursed on mother's milk—yet still delicious.
Insalata con pomodori al forno.
Fave fritte.

Trippa alla Fiorentina.
Ah, those salads, the fried fava beans—
and the gooey, drippy tomato tripe
in a fat bun leaking its red sauce.
All the scary-glorious dishes of lovers
that make the old eat young again.

SHE WAS TOO PRETTY

Suddenly, one day she was
the prettiest girl in school.
But she was too pretty, too young,
and when she turned sixteen,
the older boys gathered around her
like sharks circling a young seal,
arriving in their T-birds, their red Mustangs,
their '57 Chevrolets with hood scoops,
racing tires, and Hemi transmissions.
They wore their ducktails long,
whirlpooled their forelocks with Brylcreem,
and carried a mickey of rye
in their tight jean pockets.
They had real jobs at supermarkets.
And the girls swooned over them.
Soon she was drinking cheap wine
just like an adult, and being driven
everywhere, a blonde queen in the school.
She was too pretty, too young.

When I met her ten years later
her young body was already sagging,
bloated and ruined by wrecked cars
and alcohol and unwanted children,

and a soggy husband
no longer leading the team,
except those at the pool hall.
Her ruined skin pancaked with
makeup and pain and sad eyes,
and all the joys of the glorious
had vanished from her face.

THAT FOREVER SUMMER

These were the endless years
of my memory—I'm the butterfly
that remembers the cocoon and the caterpillar.
I put my head to the rails
listening for the forever train,
and offered a penny and a spoon,
gifts for the iron wheels to flatten.
My friends, when they weren't busy
with their circle jerks and betting
who could shoot the highest until
one juiced the chandelier,
they claimed that Apache warriors
could put their ears to the earth
and count two riders
on the way out of morning.
So I always kept my ears to the dirt,
listening for the riders, and once
in the last years of my innocence,
there was a rumbling in the ground,
and I stood up amazed
in the high, golden valley
grass of those eternal summers,
as the thundering, riderless

herd of mustangs rushed
around and past me,
galloping wild and more free
than even the memory.

THE INVISIBLE HEART

Do the dead have spirits?
They can't. There would
be too many filling the immensity.
The world is dying, in greater
and greater quantities, the dead
rising out of earthquakes
and tidal waves and heroin needles
and guns and childbirth and the virus
floating inside the lung.
The dead whirling around us,
chickens and cattle and children,
millions of spirits flying
past our startled faces.
Waves of shuddering wraiths
brushing us with the coldness
of the grave's soil and the ocean,
the fires of that last pyre.
The dead going everywhere,
flying away like rockets, comets,
waterfalls of shadows, waning flares,
meteors in the night—silent
candles fading into the forever invisible.

EXISTENCE

According to some
thoughts of Joseph Conrad.

Once I knew I lived a myth, everything else was easy,
the wash on the shore, life as it's lived,
mists in the meadows, ideas, thoughts, vanishing, appearing
    like a cougar in the canopy of trees.
    This is life?
    This is what I know?

    Yes!

Shadows without reason, without guilt, filled with desire,
shadows without morality, without hope, only awareness,
an object floating on the misty obscure waters of fantasies.

    A moment,
    a magic,
    and then it vanished.

Nothing remains except the shore mud, total mud, deep mud,
real mud that sucks us down with its reality; and there's
the sun, coming through the mist, floating above the mud
where you're stuck to the waist and considering your death.

There's only hope;
then nothing,
no sound, nothing—
mud and more mud—

the fine, ludicrous clot of existence swallowing itself.
That's when you are dead.

THE SEASON OF THE THRUSH

The birds, they sing me sweet
songs of home in their season,
and tell me where I belong,
though the years have taken this body
to strange lands and strange loves.
I've been wrong and wronged.
I wouldn't deny any of it,
the way I can't deny the Swainson's thrush
investing me with memories—
those soft, narcotic hallucinations of travel
and danger and community and conversation.
I've been a smoker, a snorter, an injector—
a hard drifter come to the highways—
a hunter of berries and bears,
and a street-tough urchin.
A dumpster diver
living by my wits—and theft.
I was the street strutting
     fire stealer,
lighting my campfires
on solitary mountains,
looking toward some kind of decency,
     honest at last,

honest and always wanting
the sap of a good life;
until knowing my final place
in the season of the thrush.

LITTLE BROWN BIRDS

Coming upon their drama—
one down, the other
standing sentry on the road—
we had no room
to move in the traffic
and I drove over
their feathered devotion.
The perfect lover waiting:
"I'll die with you, darling."

What do you think
when you drive over a bird?
Sorrow, without qualification.
Then I saw them in my mirror.
The one still standing, miraculous,
beside the fallen companion.

Little brown birds
living out their ending together.
Companions forever
in flight and death.
And when I turned the car
at the corner, I circled back
to rescue what I could

of their passion play.
Hit birds, brown birds
dying connected.

Instead, I found empty pavement.
As if they had ascended
to some greater tree
where the seeds are endless
and winter never comes, but
maybe the dead one just awoke,
undead, shook itself, and they
flew off together, another
miracle alive in the world.

TAKE OFF YOUR CLOTHES

Take off your clothes.
Drop them at your feet.
Walk naked toward me.
This is the splendour
of creatures like us.
Tomorrow, we will be dead.
Today, we will be desire.

DOMESTIC MYSTERIES OF THE KNIFE

In our kitchen she embraces the blade;
  the boning knife.
It was mine always, he thought
while she acknowledged the chicken;
she nodded, in the kitchen, at the dead bird—
ignoring him—and she considered its parts,
the boning knife held like a samurai sword,
and he was no longer there, her concentration
swallowed the kitchen as she addressed dinner—
the thigh, the drumstick, the wing, the breast,
so much variety when you have a boning knife
in your hands in the kitchen and you are ignoring him—
although he was the one who always boned the chicken
  until that day.

SHE LEFT

It's the ancient story;
your pillow is hollow
and you are gone.

When I see you in the years ahead,
if I live to see you again,
I will be wearing the green scarf.

SIGNAL FIRES

The black clouds roll over the land,
    lumpy as old meat wrongly
tossed into the compost—
    smudge fires before spring.

You burn everything.
    Wisps of smoke rise above the fog;
miniature, slow tornadoes among the mountains.

    The sun does its work—
the history of cold and raunchy baggage kept,
desire gone slack—you left me
    for the fire,
    and the fire
    is enormous, its red desire full
of paper bags and cardboard—your flesh
white as mushrooms beneath your flannel.

    The rage of the fire,
burning winter in the fog of winter.

ABOVE TIDE

Living is a festival
at the Words on the Water *festival*
—Campbell River, 2008

Cold runs the river;
warm, the heart.
The children are playing
amid the flood of memories—
rummaging in the boulders,
casting their lines
at the enormous salmon
beyond the shallows—
losing their toys,
racing and cartwheeling,
taking sides and not
taking sides.

Like old veterans we stand,
women and men, in clusters,
remembering and thrilling
        at the community
we've built with our bones,
our muscles, our desire.

A notion, almost a hope,
       captured us,
the dream of standing
in and above the tide, the view
over the orchard of our history.

This family, all the families,
we go to the river, celebrating,
       community,
and we will meet you there.

CEDAR STAIRCASE LAMENT

The honeyed wood of the stairs was warm
across from the crackle of the fire,
the jade-green throw rug sprawled on the floor,
the chinked log walls almost glowing.
Yet no one was in the room.

YELLOW MOON OVER TENACATITA

Out in the bay the great whales
spyhop and tail-slap; grandeur
still exists, and when you float
in the water you can hear them,
the mother and calf, singing
mournful songs to each other.

The pelicans fall from the sky,
awkward comedians catching fish,
while the young adults herd the hundreds
of babies into weird formations on the sea.

It's crazy with life here; La Manzanilla's market
is full of melons and tequila and senoritas,
buxom in tight white dresses,
pouting when their wide mothers
chase the boys away.

Across the bay, in Tenacatita, the hotels
are empty, the chairs along the sea-swept sea wall
scattered and forlorn. It's a recession, they say,
but the blue puffer fish still act as saintly guides
leading the way between the crags of coral,

where the saucy little stingrays touch and roll
and wriggle sensually around my legs,
breeding on the sandy bottom of the bay.

Everything here is almost as it was.
And briefly, I wonder how long
will our war on the world
hold back the crashing waves at Tenacatita?

SEVEN BULLETS TO THE BRAIN

"…a survey published in The Guardian *on Monday said
seventy-three per cent of respondents were prepared to
relinquish some freedoms in return for enhanced security."*
—*The New York Times*, August 23, 2005
(Slighly more more than one month after the assassina-
tion of the innocent Brazilian electrician, Jean Charles
de Menezes, by a police officer in the London subway.)

Was he clean, was he dirty?
Did he look like a Muslim?
I can't get the picture because
it's being erased, like the cameras
of public opinion, cluttered
with the talent of conflicting news releases.

There's the bulky overcoat,
the leaping-over-turnstiles in a subway.
The now-gone myths of official reports,
the disinformation of democracy.

*Hey, he looked dark. He must have
been a terrorist.*

But when did the war against terrorism
turn into terrorism?
When did the clink of shell casings

falling onto a dirty floor become
        the sound of freedom?

An innocent electrician is pinned down by a cop
and seven slugs are blown into his brain as he grovels
in the grease and the gum wrappers and newspapers.
This is the news, and then it is filed away; a life
sacrificed for cameras and assassins,
        recording your every movement
        and then deleting you,
        if you live in the wrong house.

LADY-BOY AT THE SIEM REAP BRIDGE

Beauty smiled at me
on the Siem Reap bridge—
guarded by the seven-headed Naga.

All her charms on display;
the platinum-blonde shimmering hair;
her high, full Khmer breasts.
The classic willow-woman waist.

Forty years ago I would have
said yes ... yes ... yes ...
just for the experience
and the joy of discovery.

But I am exhausted now
and I could only smile
and pass her some money,
before I walked away from beauty.

WE ARE THE COMET

We are the comet
that killed the dinosaur.

I look out the window,
and it's May and the thrush
has yet to return
as I turn away from the window
and look upon my luxury,
this kitchen of plenty:

coffee from scary cooperatives,
sugar from brutalized labourers,
milk from tortured cows,
salt from the mines,
bread from GMO grain.

It's a new world, magic
with plenty and temptation.

Though outside the window
thousands of songbirds are dying
in poisoned fields and suburbs
that were once good marsh.

Our farm's wild orchids have disappeared
in the twenty years since we inhabited this landscape,
devoured before they could seed
by the maws of the invading deer.
Splendid creatures converted into a pest
by colonization's rewriting of the landscape.
But blame is only a variation on stupidity.

I know I am the extinction.

LOVE AND SHIT

A homage for Patrick Lane,
after his poem, "Ten Miles in from Horsefly"

I know they are always there,
those "clear hard boards below,"
the good wood beneath the endless
manure pile of this day in this life.
It feels good, I am young, the muscles alive—
pushing-scraping-heaving the crap
into the wooden trailer for the garden.

The sun shafts through the boards of the barn
and for a moment I am blasted by a light-show
at the Retinal Circus in Vancouver with
Janis Joplin belting out her now ancient love
in the shadows of black light and amoebas.

Every sun-bolt in the barn creates
a zone of hoarded wealth—flooding
the bench and its jars of screws.
The brass, the stainless steel, the zinc.
Each molten gold and silver like a treasure
where we would least expect it.
I am Blackbeard and Captain Morgan,
pirate thieves of light and life.

I am chasing the mystery, the magic, the reality,
sweating among the horseflies, lost, excavating
the soft intestinal release and tangled hay.
Then suddenly I hit the boards and look down
at the real mystery, the flash of lives never known,
a gold ring in the manure pile.

READING CATULLUS
for Patrick

Reading Catullus and weeping at the dawn
of my dying, the slow slow going that
is my death. Hail and Farewell, brother.
We got smashed, the blue sky rolled
over our weak tiny bodies, and our love,
though we endured close to fifty years together.
I'm going to the other side, shoulders
and defiance intact. I'll meet you there, following
you from the beach to the interior to the beach again,
my love, my friend, my lost one. I'm going.
Farewell and Hello. I'm on my way. Raging.
Already I see you at the burning gate.

THOSE OLD VARIATIONS

(1)

THE FUNDAMENTALIST

The young man writhed
with blood and fury, feeding
on the politics of purity,
too quick to note
the failings of his friends
and the lovers that left
his bed and his life. He
demanded perfect attention,
a perfect world, perfect
in its perfect details,
until he grew old, witnessing
the same battles forever
repeating themselves
in his bed and on the borders.
But he was a clever creep,
and so he learned how to add
a little honey to his sting.

(2)

BOY-CHILD-OLD-MAN-MIRROR-TRICK

Look into the image of you, boy-child,
the endless eyelashes, the floating wild hair
draped down to your ass.
The long bones of hormones
that didn't stop growing
until the doctors whacked you with chemicals.

Boy child, you were the wind on the road,
stopped suddenly by the purple asters,
or the smile of the waiter-girl
whose legs stretched down to the floor,
and you spent years buying
a thousand hot beef sandwiches
so you could love her legs
and dream of the cascading
premature silver hair of her
nineteen years in the world,
hair that touched your mouth
when she leaned over the table
to refill the foul coffee
you drank to bring her back.

So turn again to the mirror and stare
at the thickened face of your age,
and smile and remember the now nearly
ancient, silver-haired waitress of your desires.

(3)

OLD MAN'S HANDS

I sit at the table and see
an old man's hands. They are
my hands, bony, veined, even wrinkled.
What happened, what happened
to the hope, the years that passed?
Time is what happened, glorious time.
Delicious time. So much wonder and learning
that's still left me useless,
watching your love grow distant,
watching you grow lost,
beyond the decades of our love,
watching you find me a subject of sorrow,
watching you at the dinner table,
like a fifteen-year-old child
who believes everything about me
can be done better, can be done
with a fifteen-year-old child's wisdom.
But you are not fifteen and you have seen
me fail, seen me fall, seen me collapse
in the ginger that life is, the foliage, the teeth,
of the world that chews us up—
when I needed beating, and even

the many more beatings I didn't deserve.
Now, outside, the magnolia petals
and the almond blossoms are wind,
littering the green crazy-green field
with the colour of the season.
You saw everything, and now you are looking
at my old hands with contempt
and I have no answer for those hands.

(4)

OLD DOG
for Olive

She's dying, my dog
a grey-muzzled,
black muscled
big bullet of a dog.
She broke her back
chasing a racoon up a tree
and survived the arthritis
for the last five years.
Now she leans against my thigh
trembling, full of spinal agony,
all hungry to live.

(5)

GENTLY, THAT GENTLE ONE WENT

Gently, that gentle one went.
A good New Year's dinner,
a touch of indigestion.
Sixty years old but trim
and hard-working and healthy,
maybe heartburned from too fine a meal.
She followed him to their bedroom.
He lay down and let out a big sigh,
and the sigh was his last breath.
Sixty short years, a talented, quiet man
alone on his bed with his wife—
stunned, and gazing upon him,
mouth quivering at the years, their lives...
O astonishing astonishing world!

FALLING FORWARD

There he is, the rooster boy
gaunt with death,
a victim of the concentration camp
called life in this world.

He was an ugly baby—
into everything, whacking
his bathtub, yanking
the pots out of the cupboard.

Falling, endlessly falling
off steps, chairs, ladders, beds—
falling into the whirlpool.

Then he was a pretty young man,
still falling, falling, falling into love,
language, the good companions,
falling into the starry whirlpool.

He grew fat, still falling,
falling for the big easy, falling
into middle age and then scrawny old age
that came faster than a night train.

Now he's spavined, and gussied
by the undertaker's art, as pretty
as you can make death.

But the smile and the shining eyes,
that fresh life is gone out of the husk,
which will soon be falling
into the fire of its own ashes.

(7)

OLD LOVE

Once it was love
and love was all she wanted,
waltzing endless into the mists,
but history changes the body
into the desire that this history
makes comic book
with romance and lush fantasies.
She awoke and he was missing,
only the shell remained beside her,
scary, hollow, unloving.

Is this our future she asked
when she looked into his face
of disdain and distance?

This thick, saggy flesh?
A wrinkled, hollow bag?
Empty is the container—
the dance of love infected with age.

REFLECTION IN THE EYE OF AN OLD MAN

The years, they look good,
a mind as sharp as a punk kid,
still filled with *all-or-nothing*,
and then the surprise,
the recognition; there you are,
an old man drinking
whiskey in a cracked glass.

THE OLD POET LIES DYING

I knew him in the swagger
of his prime, and then
the pride of middle age,
and now I know the humbling
illness of his late years.
I can't say I knew him well
but I followed him
in the adventures of the word.
He had a quality that
you could only call ...
"a quality"—the stiff back
of hard-work and hard-thinking.
A quality that, even
shrunk and fading,
stands higher than I can stand.

WE GOT OLD

They say youth is wasted
on the young, but we did
our share of damage. I wrecked
the place for plenty years
before I began rebuilding it.

We were so hot, so firey
with our glorious hair and weird
clothes and music and rebellion
that ended up becoming advertising slogans.
Ah well, the end is never
what you want; it's what happens,
and now our eyes are failing,
and our bellies are filling,
and our teeth are falling out,
and several friends need walkers,
but some of us still have the wild hearts
of crazed nineteen-year-old children.

WAITING FOR THE TIGER

Last report from inside the belly of the beast.

Long ago they said the tiger was on the mountain,
moving down through the savannah.
We watched for him when we stood
on our porches or when the grass grew high
until everything disappeared into the ravine.
He was the strangest tiger. Sometimes
you caught a glimpse beside
the road in traffic jams
and wondered—Was that the tiger?

I knew he was coming closer
when my bones began to howl
in the dawn's circus of light.
I knew he was around once
my friends began to disappear.
There were shadows and sad feasts
where kind words praised the lost.
And children with wide eyes
soon learned the meaning of tiger.

I knew he had come this morning.
I knew these were my last thoughts
in the thicket of noise and light,

bright stripes among green fronds.
There was the click of the breaking.
It was almost gentle, the air streaming,
this rich life going, a defiant bird singing,
as the tiger walked up the hill
with my neck in his jaws.

SOLSTICE AT SIXTY

Now that the sun of my setting
approaches the last rise and fall
marking the suns of my seasons—
the frosty breaths of this solstice
and the light pouring winter
into the lake of limpid water—
I count every morning and night.
Blue dark, exquisite darkness
in the deeps of the water,
the deeps of this dark,
those brilliant stars
punched into the night's black fabric.

Then came the solstice eclipse,
342 years of waiting, and I waited.
It was a cloudy night, muck and rain before
the mist cleared and the moon
shook off her sepia dreadlocks,
Blood-headed moon, a brief flash
between 11:45 and 12:15.
A total eclipse; then pale copper on the moon.
I turned around and everyone had left for bed,
easy companions in an easy world. Yet when
the moon comes late my friends disappear.

But if the aged go to ashes
the young go to the light.
Bright and more bright the day after,
all their joys and the dumb promise
of spring following the snow.

The threat of darkness only means
light and birth and love will follow,
the crazy lustrous jewels of the world
blazing in the ashes of my bones
my father's bones, history's bones.
Light growing longer by the minute now.
Every thing and any thing that's lovely—
the sorcery that's the urgent tomorrow—
catkins and flowers and calving grounds,
children and young dogs and seeds—
all the gifts of the summer day arriving.

BURNING ME

They say it's easier on the earth
to be buried within the earth.
But I'm going to be burned.
I've done my green work
so I'll give back a little smoke—
dioxins, furans, PCBs,
the crap pumped into me
by the corporate oligarchy.
Then you can scatter
my silver bones and ashes
in the sea off Rebecca Spit,
the peninsula of my island childhood.
And I want you to follow me into ash,
follow me, follow me down.
We'll feed the fish and moon snails,
and scale the food chain.
We will dive with whales,
swim with the grilse
and spiny urchin shamble,
or crab walk beside the sea cucumber;
then Tyee salmon ascend
the rivers to face the great bear.
When my brains are eaten
and belly scooped out, I'll feed
the giant cedar and spruce and fir.

I will become lumber
and you'll live in my cities.
And I want you to accompany me,
darling, when it's your turn to die—
burn bright and beautiful
my bone and ash girl—
accompany me, accompany me down
when your time comes to join
the circle of sea and sky and land,
and we'll circle the circle together.
You will salmon the slow rivers
of the fields of the valley
and I'll fertilize the good dirt,
and the flowers will be bright with me.
I'll become bean and melon and tulip.
I will never leave you, darling.
I will be totally here,
everywhere, all the time.
Around you, surrounding you
the way you surrounded me
in our life together.

And I want you to follow me,
follow me, follow me down
until we are together all around.

BLUE

Blue, I hardly know you,
       nor how important you are.
           Human
       blue of my blue jeans
       from new to ruins.

Blue of teal skies.
       Blue of original sorrow.
           Blue of the vein on her white breast.
       Blue of the river
           before it met the muddy water
               of another river.
Blue in her eyes
       before I knew love was complicated.
Blue of how I learned that complication.
           Blue of glaciers that are ancient
       even as they wash away.
Blue of my brave Chevy pickup
       that I drove into the ground.

O blue, you have done me wrong,
    given me the *blue mind*
        of a man who must live near water,

    shone too much for me, made me
dive into you, blue.
    O blue, I want you, blue....

I WHO

I who once was brave.
I who once was beautiful.
I who strode into the ranks
of the ugly and the mean and the twisted,
and heaved their biting teeth backwards.

I who once wore my hair down to my hips,
and washed and brushed it before battle.
I who was knocked into the dust.
I who rose again and was knocked down again.
I who received the stiletto from my lover, between the first
and the second rib, when I was washing my hair,
while blinded by my vanity and my crazy purpose.

I who was a fool for love without end.
I who was a fool who wanted to save the city
that never wanted to be saved.
I who once fought the gods
while my army sold itself to the corporations
and I turned to witness only emptiness behind me.
I who was a fool with my marvelous hair
tangled in the mud and shit and blood.
I who chewed on the crap of my dying.

I who fell for you and would fall again,
over and over again, my love. I who could
only crash into the ecstasy of this collapse,
ravished by my own pathetic death.

DID YOU GO TOO FAR?

"I think we led safer lives when we played around with knives."
—John Mann, Spirit of the West

There's a bitterness in the air, my generation
was naive and actually believed in a future.
Then they became jelly and bought luxury houses.
Well, I still believe, and I run with the wild
in the forest paths of existence; some of us still
run, run those forest paths, run for nowhere.

I grew up bloodied and smacked
and then I came back and said,
"You can smack me again," because
I'm still going to run down that forest path
to oblivion. I'm alive. I'm alive.
        Until I am dead.
I wander lost among the planetary stardust
of decaying bodies, plant and animal,
the blooms of the green earth and birth.
        I understand less every day,
and I thrill at the discoveries of my ignorance.
I have lived defying my bones and leaps
into space that were never possible, jumps
I'm paying for with these bones now.
I'm celebrating the fucked, the beautiful,

the lost—with energy, I write these words
only for those who know that going too far
is not going far enough.

Brian Brett is a poet, fictionist, memoirist, journalist and former chair of the Writers' Union of Canada.

Brett's genetic disorder, the rare Kallmann Syndrome, was apparent at birth, yet it went undiagnosed and untreated until he was 20. The failure to go through puberty until his 20s, and his mistreatment because of his ladyboy appearance, led him to a lifetime of work as an activist supporting local communities and social issues, both national and international, and the literary world, mainly through The Writers Union of Canada.

When he was 17, Cecil Reid, his English teacher (later a Bella Bella Heiltsuk chief), with a master's degree in classics, set the stage for Brett writing his world – sideways to the academic poetry of today. Reid illuminated the path of "rebellion and poetry and knowledge" for two years while Brett, with irony and fierceness, inhaled his school teacher's introduction to world literature before finding his own wandering path.

Brett's 14 wildly diverse books that followed include the poems of *The Colour of Bones in a Stream*; the genre bending novel, *Coyote: A Mystery*; the *Globe* book-of-the year memoir, *Uproar's Your Only Music*; his best-selling *Trauma Farm: A Rebel History of Rural Life* (which won numerous prizes, including the Writers' Trust Award for best book of Canadian non-fiction in 2010); and an earlier version of *To Your Scattered Bodies Go* won the CBC Poetry Prize. His latest collection of poems is *The*

Wind River Variations. The final book in his trilogy of memoirs, the award-winning *Tuco and the Scattershot World: A Life with Birds*, was published in 2015. He is also the recipient of the Lieutenant General's Award for Lifetime Achievement, and the Matt Cohen Lifetime Achievement Award. He is currently finishing a new novel, a new memoir, and always, new poems.

Some of these poems have appeared in the following newspapers, literary magazines, and anthologies: *The Victoria Times Colonist, The Tyee, The Antigonish Review, EXILE Quarterly, Refugium: Poems of the Pacific, Sweet Water: Poems for the Watershed, Voicing Suicide*, and *Sustenance: Writers from BC and Beyond on the Subject of Food*.

A note about the cover's author photo: *Valentine's Day Massacre* is not your standard portrait, but I like it, and I like its history – taken on Valentine's Day, it was when I was (incorrectly!) informed I had terminal, inoperable liver cancer. Those roses I bought for myself died within a day.